Becky's Poems

Written by **Rebecca Hardison Smith**

Illustrations by **Mary Barrows**

J2B Publishing LLC, Pomfret, MD

Becky's Poems

Written by Rebecca Hardison Smith
Illustrations by Mary Barrows
Design/Layout by James Burd Brewster and Mary Barrows

Published by J2B Publishing LLC
4251 Columbia Park Road
Pomfret, MD 20675
GladToDoIt@gmail.com

ISBN: 978-1941927274
All rights reserved.

Copyright 2015 by Rebecca Hardison Smith

Illustrations Copyright 2015 by Mary Barrows

No part of this publication may be reproduced, stored in a retrieval system, or transmitted in any form or by any means—for example, electronic, photocopy, recording—without prior written permission of the publisher. The only exception is brief quotations for reviews. For information address: J2B Publishing LLC

Becky's Poems

Written by **Rebecca Hardison Smith**

Illustrations by **Mary Barrows**

J2B Publishing LLC, Pomfret, MD

I dedicate this book to my family.

Contents:

The Steeple	1
Gethesemane	3
Our Flag	5
Perry Long's Pickles	6
Our Faithful School Janitor	8
Mama Sang	11
Rainbow	12
The Fallen Oak	15
Purple Snow	16
Cora's "Posthumous" Trip	17
Dreams	18
Mrs. Armstrong	20
Laura Spivey's Birds	21
Donald's House	22
Margaret's Fruit Cake	23
Wake Up America	25
Don Jr's Whooping Cough	27
Santa's Trip	29
I Love Christmas	30
The Old Sounder	32
Pig Tails	35

Author's Acknowledgements

I would like to thank family members and friends who encouraged me to have my poems published, especially my dear ninety year old friend, Laura Spivey, who said to me, "Just do it!"

My special thanks to J2B Publishing who made it so easy.

Introduction

I have always loved to write poems. I think it's fun and a perfect way to recall people from my past. It seems to bring them back to me. Writing about serious subjects can be a challenge, but it's all a joy for me.

The Steeple

Our church sits on a corner and
Its steeple reaches high.
It seems to call and beckon
To each one passing by.

It calls, "Come in and join us.
Come and sit a spell.
And listen to our preacher;
He has a story to tell."

He tells us of God's Mighty Power,
And of Salvation full and free.
He tells us of God's only Son,
Who died upon a tree.

He speaks of James and John and Simon.
Just to name a few.
As we all sit and listen,
On our wooden pews.

When the sermon is over,
And you go out to leave this place.
Stop and look at the steeple.
It's pointing at God's face.

Gethesemane

I left Him in the Garden,
And ran and hid behind a tree.
The Roman soldiers came,
And found Him praying on his knees.

My fear just overtook me,
As I retreated into the dark.
My Lord looked over at me,
And it almost broke my heart.

The thorns they later placed upon Him,
Should have pierced my head instead.
My blackened heart condemned me,
And I wished that I was dead.

If ever again He should ask me,
With Him to abide.
I'll jump for joy and run to Him,
And never leave his side.

Our Flag

I saw "Old Glory" on the ground,
And rushed to pick her up.
She was covered in dirty leaves-
A little mud and soot.

I shook her and unfurled her,
And placed her in her stand.
And watched her pleats go back and forth,
It was truly grand.

To see her beauty and her pride,
And all her colors true.
The beauty and the majesty
Of the red, the white, the blue.

Perry Long's Pickles

I know a man named Perry,
Who makes delicious pickles.
Every time he shares them,
We are all so tickled.

They're tart and firm and tangy-
We just can't get enough.
I tried to make them one day,
But mine weren't "up to snuff."

I tried to sneak his recipe,
And follow his directions.
I shared them with my neighbors,
And only got rejections.

So we'll depend on Perry,
To continue with his treat.
Because I am here to tell you,
Perry's pickles can't be beat!

Our Faithful School Janitor

Old Jack Farley

was a real good man.

He kept our school house

spic and span.

He got up early

every morn,

to stoke the fires

that kept us warm.

He was real loyal,

he was true blue.

He probably didn't earn

one twenty-two.

And he raised "Old Glory"

every morn

To remind us kids

where we were born.

Mama Sang

Mama sang "Heavenly Sunshine"
as she stood at the ironing board.

She sang "Bringing in the Sheaves"
as she mopped the kitchen floor.

While she cooked our supper,
she sang "Amazing Grace."

Sang it every time,
with a smile upon her face.

She sang "Victory in Jesus,"
hanging clothes on the old clothes line.

Oh, how I'd love to hear her,
sing a song just one more time.

Rainbow

We went out to the middle of the Galilee,
A sea so beautiful and calm.
The boat was filled with hopeful souls-
Seeking a healing balm.

Our Bibles were open, our leader stood
And read the words we needed.
The wisest words we ever heard,
They needed to be heeded.

As we sat, a rainbow came,
And spread across the sky -
A blessing sent by God I'm sure,
A blessing for our eyes.

Such things, I know,
we don't deserve,
But they stop
and make us think.
The gift He sent that perfect day,
I'm sure, was just a "God Wink."

The Fallen Oak

I took a trip to see a friend,
And much to my surprise.
I heard a thud and felt a thump,
And ran to look outside

    A mighty oak had pulled a joke,
    And fell across the street.
    It wasn't satisfied with that.
    It made a truck a "heap."

        So anytime the wind is howling,
        It's better to take heed.
        Cause mighty oaks, as we all know,
        Got started as a seed.

Purple Snow

I looked out my door one day,

And thought I saw purple snow;

Maybe Lavender or Lilac,

For all I know.

So, I went outside to get a closer look,

And almost had hysteria;

When suddenly I realized,

It was just Wisteria.

Cora's "Posthumous" Trip

I taught my kids to be frugal,
To save a "buck" or two.
Times were getting harder,
This I knew was true.

I must have taught them well,
And If I could, I'd holler,
"You kids will go to any length,
Just to save a dollar!"

Also, I think they went too far,
Just to save some bucks,
When they took me to Carolina,
In a rental truck.

When I reach the Pearly Gates,
When Saint Pete and I greet each other,
I'll smile and walk on in and yell,
"Lord, I'm glad that's over!"

Dreams

You're a shadow in my heart,
A dream from long ago.
I sit for hours and think of you,
Of thoughts I can't let go.

Most every night I dream of you,
And wake up very sad;
Until our children come to me,
And soon again, I'm glad.

Mrs. Armstrong

Old Mrs. Armstrong
 was cranky and crotchety.
Sometimes she acted
 as mean as a Nazi.

In her class,
 you'd better sit up and listen,
and not start a sentence,
 with a preposition.

Or she might smack your head,
or slap you on your hand.
I saw her do that once,
to Bobby Bland.

Nooooo, she didn't hit him,
not even one time,
But, I needed his name
to make this poem rhyme.

Laura Spivey's Doves

I love my little garden,
Just outside my door.
It makes me very happy,
I couldn't ask for more.

There are Blue Jays and Cardinals,
 And Robins and Sparrows.
I enjoy them so much,
I could watch them for hours.

But the ones I love, are the beautiful doves.

Their cooing is soothing.
They are probably wooing,
A dove on another limb.

So take time to listen,
Or you will be missin',
A serenade as sweet as a hymn.

Donald's House

I built a castle on a creek.
It didn't lean, it didn't leak.
The thing I liked about it most,
As I stood against its pillar posts,
Were its shiny doors and brand new floors.

On the front porch I drank Champagne.
On the back porch I counted change.
Out front,
I had the Rockafellows and the Pruitts.
Out back,
Old Jack Fowler and the Hewetts.

Out front - Caviar
Out back - old guitar
I have the best of two worlds,
So, I'll tip my hat.
Now, what in the heck, do you think of that?

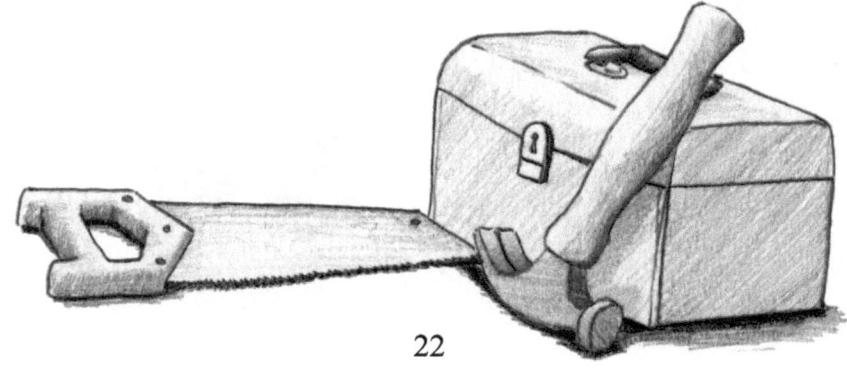

Margaret's Fruit Cake

I love fruit cake.

It's the one thing I adore.

Once I dropped a piece,

And ate it off the floor.

The nuts, the fruit, the sugar, the spice,

I gotta tell you, I can't eat just one slice.

To non-fruit cake lovers,

To this I can attest.

You've got to try my sister's,

It's the very best!!

Wake Up America!

I had a dream.
It upset me so.
In the dream I asked,
"Where did my country go?"

The laws, and morals, and
rules were weak,
As if we had lost
our winning streak.

The schools were dangerous,
Teachers received no respect-
Our government officials said,
"What the heck,"
Just so we get our weekly check.

China, Russia, or who knows who,
Could fly their flag above our schools.

I woke up in a sweaty pool,
How long are we to be the fools?

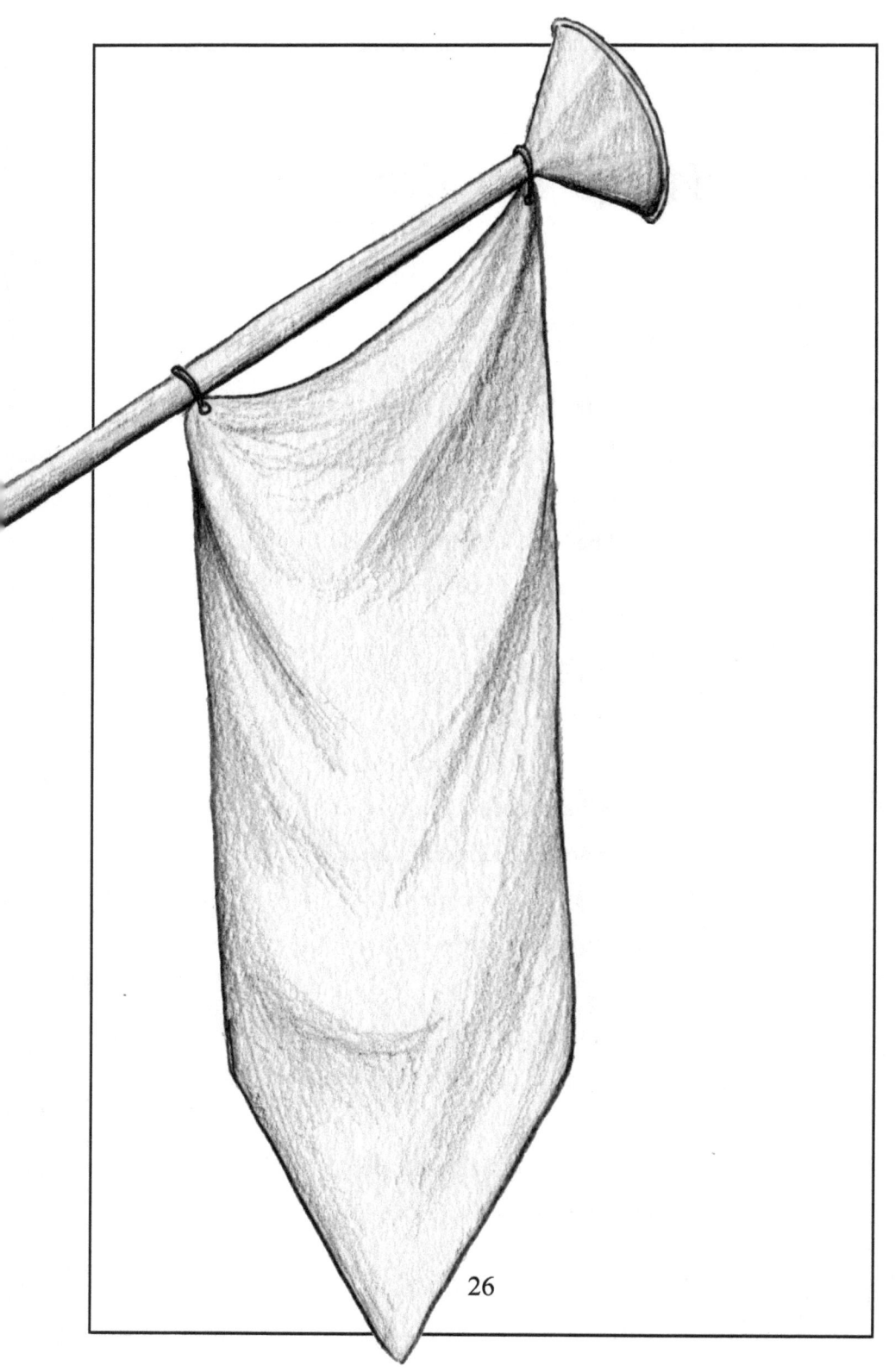

Don Jr's Whooping Cough

I remember the day you were born.

I wanted to blow a horn,

to announce the day

you came our way,

and wish you a very long stay.

The "Doodle Bug" scar on your neck

reminded us, "Oh Heck"

how scared we were that day

you could have gone away,

But was saved by a Doc with a "trach".

Santa's Trip

Santa's waiting in his sleigh,

Waiting to take off.

He nearly almost couldn't go,

Because he had an awful cough.

So Mrs. Claus mixed a brew, and put it in his tea.

He felt so good, he loaded up,

And headed through the trees.

So look beneath your Christmas tree.

You'll find your toys are there.

Santa Claus is real you see,

To this I'll surely swear.

I Love Christmas!

Happy days are here again.

Yes, it's Christmas Time!

Carolers singing on the porch,

This time of the year is fine!

      Mistletoe above the door,

      For those who want a kiss.

      I'll rush right over,

      On my toes,

      This I wouldn't miss.

           I hope your Holiday is perfect,

           And I'm sure that it will be.

           Because we live in America,

           Land of the brave and free.

God Bless America And Merry Christmas!!

The Old "Sounder"

He got up every morning and headed to the docks.

He would take his boat around the bend,

And hope to catch some "spots."

He sat sometimes for hours on end,

And only caught some Shad.

But fish are fish and all are good,

So for Shad he was even glad.

He preferred a foot-long Flounder,

To stuff with some shrimp and crumbs.

A treat you couldn't imagine,

Unless you'd eaten some.

His oyster roasts were always great,

Once he even found a pearl.

He put it on a silver chain,

And gave it to his girl.

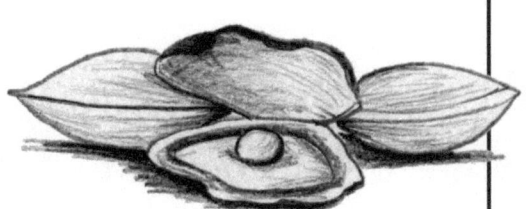

He also loved delicious clams,

He could find them with his toes.

He would take them home and line then up,

And wash them with a hose.

Then he would put them on the stove,

And watch them open up.

And dip them in garlic butter,

And soon begin to sup.

Hot corn bread from the oven-

With butter he would splash.

And tell everyone at the table,

"Forget about Calabash!!"

Pig Tails

I was sitting at my desk at school,
Catching up on my work.
I was concentrating on my book –
When my pig tail got a jerk.

I turned around and thought I'd find
A classmate sitting there.
But saw my teacher, Mrs. Bond,
And then I heard a tear.

She ripped my book completely up –
It shook me to my bones.
Then yelled at me, right to my face –
"Leave the comic books at home!"

The Author

Rebecca Hardison Smith was born and raised in Wilmington, NC. She is a widow with two sons and a daughter; James, Charles and Kelly, and six beautiful grandchildren; James, Sean, Lauren, Brook, Ivy and Cole. Her hobbies are writing poems, working crossword puzzles, playing her piano, and traveling.

She has had the opportunity to travel to Israel, France, England, Belize, Mexico, and the Bahamas. She hopes to go to Italy next.

Her poems are based on people and events in her life; some political, some religious, and some humorous (her favorites). She hopes to write another book of poems in the near future.

The Illustrator

Mary Barrows is a freelance illustrator from the small town of Walkerville, MD. Since she was old enough to hold a pencil, she has been drawing pictures of her favorite stories, and she hasn't stopped yet. She is the second oldest of six kids with a passion for children's books and fantasy stories. When she isn't illustrating, Mary loves to read, play basketball, and mess around on her guitar.

www.ingramcontent.com/pod-product-compliance
Lightning Source LLC
Chambersburg PA
CBHW052041280426
43661CB00084B/14